memoir
Book 2026

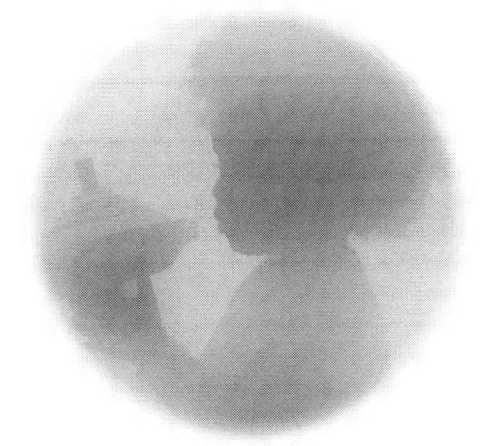

TRANSLUCENT

A MEMOIR & SURVIVAL GUIDE FOR RAISING KIDS
WITH INVISIBLE NEEDS THE SYSTEM MISSES,
THE WORLD JUDGES AND KAREN SIDE-EYES AT THE CHECKOUT

NY M JONES

Jones
& Inc Press
From Paper to Purpose

TRANSLUCENT
A Memoir & Survival Guide for Raising Kids with Invisible Needs the System Misses, the World Judges and Karen Side-Eyes at the Checkout
© 2025 **Ny M Jones**

First published in the United Kingdom by
Jones and Inc Press, December 2025

Editor: Nyesha Jones

Cover Design: Nyesha Jones

ISBN: 978-1-0369-6784-0

Printed in the United Kingdom

For permissions, inquiries, or media contact:
info@jonesandincpress.com

British Library Cataloguing in Publication Data:
A catalogue record for this book is available from the British Library.

Dedication

For Houdini,

You are light in its purest form, unshaped by the world, yet shaping it by your being.
You came translucent, to teach me, and all who see you, that truth does not need fixing, only witnessing.
This book is not about you, but through you.
It is my honour to be your voice until the world learns to hear your own.

Blessing

May these words travel only where they are welcomed.
May they serve as mirrors for those who need to remember compassion.
May they open doors of understanding for children like Houdini, and windows of release for parents who carry silent weight.
May no energy of judgement, envy, or distortion cling to these pages.
May the good generated here ripple outward, returning in multiplied form to Houdini's journey and to all families who walk beside him.

TRANSLUCENT

(/tranz'luːs(ə)nt/)

Allowing light to pass through, but diffusing it so that persons, objects, etc., on the other side are not clearly visible.

Oxford English Dictionary (OED)

Author's Note

This book is a lived account of parenting a child whose needs are often **translucent**. When I say Translucent, I mean needs that are partly visible, partly hidden; seen in flashes, missed in passing, and easily misunderstood.

I'm not a clinician and this is not medical advice. The terms I use include Translucent Needs, Stimming, Elopement and Sleep-Linked Avoidance. These are plain-language bridges between what families live and what services record. They are descriptive, not diagnostic.

Every child is different. My son's profiles and stories are shared with care; identifying details are altered to protect privacy. Where I reference systems, I do so from a UK, Black British, single-parent lens; your experience may look different. If the language here helps you find your own words for referrals, meetings, or simply for yourself, take it. If it doesn't, leave it.

Most of all, this is a book about recognition. If you're raising a "Houdini," I hope these pages make you feel less alone. If you're a professional, I hope they help you see what families carry between appointments.

INTRODUCTION
TRANSLUCENT

"I'm not hidden. You're just looking
with the wrong light"

Introduction
Translucent

The way I'm about to lay my life bare for you all, the front cover should really have been a picture of me butt-arse naked.
But I'm not a "nudes-taking" type of girl, so I'll do the striptease with my words.

To them, at a glance, it's just a cute kid on a swing. To me, in a blink, it's a whole operation you can't see. Like frosted bathroom glass, you know something's there, but you don't get the whole picture. He's not invisible or opaque. He does not have an obvious disability (transparent), but there are cracks of light shining through if you know where to look: the bare feet in February, the blank stares when someone says his name, the swing acrobatics. Unless you live with him, you'll miss the extent of it.

This book shows you the parts most people miss.

You've probably never heard the word *Translucent* used like this before. To be honest, there will be a few things in here you've probably never heard someone say out loud for the first time. But we'll start here.

My son's needs are translucent.

In this book, you'll see me use the word disability here only to give you a contrast. I prefer the term *Addability,* my personal reframing rather than a clinical term. I use it as a lens of recognition, not a prescription for anyone else's language.

I don't make a practice of pointing out shortcomings. Instead, I invite you to see what lies beyond the surface, the additions within what others might call limitations. That is where the magic shows up. Like any real magic, it only works when the rules are in place. When you understand the needs, you create the safety that allows the wonder to unfold.

Addability is not denial of disability. It is the refusal to reduce a person to their perceived lacks. It recognises that within every so-called limitation is a different kind of brilliance. Where others see delays, we see depth. Where others see deficit, we see dimension. *Addability* does not erase need; it dignifies it.

So, when I talk about *Translucent Needs* throughout the chapters, this is the frame I want you to hold.

I know how hard it can be to find the words. To sit across from a doctor, a teacher, a social worker, and try to explain what you live every single day. To fill out a form with boxes that never seem to fit your child. To wonder if maybe you're the only one who notices the nuances.

The needs are also for the people who stare, the ones who think it's bad behaviour, poor parenting, or chaos with no cause. Sometimes what looks like defiance is actually a medical need.
And they're for the professionals too. So, they can see the contrast between our language and theirs. Between the metaphors we use to survive and the clinical notes they write in reports.

If you recognise parts of your own story in mine, and you struggle to articulate what that looks like, these descriptions might give you the words you need. Whether it's for a referral, an assessment, a conversation with a professional, or simply for yourself.

You'll also notice that at no point will I label his condition or potential diagnosis. Because the truth is, the label doesn't matter. That label could look different in every child who carries it. Yes, there are commonalities of need, but the real gem isn't in knowing the name. It's in recognising the *how* and the *why*. Because that visibility? That's what changes their world.

I'm not handing out medical advice. I'm handing out recognition. Now that you know what I mean by translucent, let's get into what it looks like.

CHAPTER 1

HIDDEN CHAOS

"If it looks like chaos to you, it's choreography to me."

Chapter 1
The Hidden Chaos

It's February, which means every other child in the park is bundled in coats, hats, and footwear. My son, however, is barefoot in the swing, grinning like he's on a tropical beach. The 'rub your feet when the swing comes in' game we've had going for the last twenty minutes is my final attempt to do more than Rose did for Jack on that door; and his little toes feel like the iceberg that sank the ship.

1. *Translucent Need: **Sensory Seeking Behaviours***

I've given up the battle over socks and shoes. He wins every time, and frankly, I don't have the energy to negotiate with a three-year-old Houdini.

Meanwhile, on the other side of the park, his sister is dangling from a climbing frame like a circus act, looking at me for approval, her fingers gripping the cold metal, legs swinging, and a squeal of excitement escaping her. She will not stop screaming "MUM!" until I gesture some acknowledgement of her *'amazing dangerousness.'*

I vaguely make out that she is upside down from the silhouette of her braids sweeping the floor as she is waving, because transparent, translucent, or opaque, some things are universal. All kids want their moment, so with a grimace, I give her hers, a quick cheer: "Amazing, Hun! ... But be careful."

I also utter a quick prayer under my breath as I'm half-blind, and with Houdini's suggestion that my glasses are better suited to a case than my face, it's safer not to see the extra metres than going toe-to-toe with the baby from *Pixar's The Incredibles* and his death grip.

2. *Translucent Need: **Motor Extremes***

Sometimes it feels like the whole world is blurred on purpose. So, I can't actually see in detail how dangerous the *'amazing dangerousness'* I've just applauded really is, hence why I called on the 'big man upstairs'.

I also can't take a few steps for better sight because my hands are locked on the swing chain, making sure he doesn't suddenly go full Tarzan and hurl himself out into mid-air.

3. Translucent Need: **Risk Tolerance and Thrill-Seeking**

And here's the irony: if he did fall, the fact he *'fell'* would be his biggest concern, not the *'impact'* of collision or the prospect of going translucent to transparent, as his pain threshold is set at whatever the highest mark is on the test.

He very rarely expresses that he is hurt. I mean, this kid body-slams concrete freewill; yet, as nonsensical as this sounds, he is still extremely cautious, a proper little control freak. That paradox runs through him: fearless and cautious in the same breath. He tests gravity like he doesn't care, then demands the rules bend his way.

But once he makes it back on two feet, you'd best believe he's off… and unless Usain Bolt happens to be in the park, it's going to take a good twenty metres to catch him. In that sprint, the world narrows to just him: the chase, the rescue, the tunnel vision. And the second I dare to look away? There it is again: her scream cutting through, *"MUM! Look at me."*

The lady pushing the swing next to us tries to get his attention with a big wave and that exaggerated "hi there!" voice people save for toddlers. He looks straight past her as though she's a lamppost. She even tries again, eyebrows raised, like she's auditioning for *CBeebies.* Cue the commentary:
"I guess he's not in the mood to talk to me, is he?" Now add an awkward giggle: "I don't think he likes me much."

I bite my tongue for a second, because inside I'm thinking: *'Ya think? … The day we've had, I'm not even in the mood to like you much right now… much less him,'* and honestly, her attempt at small talk is just another note in the orchestra of overload.

Between my daughter's shrieks that demand constant attention, the octave between her happy screams and *'I've mashed up myself'* is paper-thin, and the clatter of swings, my head is already ringing.

4. *Translucent Need:* **Parent Sensory Load**

Under my breath, I'm muttering: *'Babe, he has never spoken to me, and I've been wiping his arse for three years, so what magic do you think you've got?'*

I know she is being polite because I was once her. Just trying to be polite and bond with another mum who unknowingly was dealing with translucent needs, hers and the child's. No visible signs of a struggle, in fact, a smile that only encouraged me to keep talking.

I mean, how was she to know he is not interested in people when it seemed so natural to her? His giggles did not let her know that her chances of a *'Hi'* back sat somewhere between zero and me winning the lottery.

I would like to explain to her that communication with Houdini doesn't come in pointing or words. It comes in dragging. He will take your hand and forcefully push or pull you towards what he wants: the fridge for a sandwich, the dishwasher for juice, the oven if he's after nuggets. And when you get it right? He does this little flap-and-bounce routine, like joy exploding through his body, approval in motion. It's his way of saying, *"You got it."*
The same one she sees every time the swing comes in.

5. *Translucent Need:* **Social and Communication Style**

But what actually leaves my mouth is the easy version: *"He's like that with everyone; it's defo not you."* Because I'm an empath and I get how she feels, and honestly, because it's easier than launching into an explanation that will probably end with: *"Oh, my cousin's neighbour's son was like that, and now he's fine."*

When the truth is, he is not your cousin's neighbour's son; he is three with a developmental age of around 18 months, the strength of 18 years, and not your unsolicited TED Talk, Karen.

With familiar people, his communication is easier to feel, literally. If you're in his circle, he won't smile, he won't even glance your way, but he'll drag you to where he needs you. If you resist? Good luck. His strength and charisma will win.

Strangers see silence, insiders see charisma. That's the blur a quick conversation can't capture: the overlap between a label and a lived child, between a diagnosis and how it actually shows up in him.

And here's where I learned my sharpest tool: communication isn't just about explaining him, it's about protecting me. Survival of the fittest is about adapting to your surroundings, and my conversations adapt based on how safe I feel and the energy I have. I also weigh how heavy my problems feel to the shoulders I lean them on, and that sets my tone. I often turn to humour; part deflection, part truth. How I speak shifts depending on who's listening:

6. *Translucent Need: **Parent Communication Strategies***

To a friend, it lands as soft truths: "I know he looks calm right now, but this is not the same version of him I have at 3am when he's swinging off the lampshade in the dark, and we have to be up at 7."

Us enduring helpful Karens at the swings isn't just for fun; they save the lives of lampshades and us surviving the night.

With relatives, its truth, banter, or both: "He looks fine because I'm not. I've spent half my night googling hacks to get the smell of *Hackney City Farm's* animals out of my carpet and furniture before one of you unexpectedly visits and thinks I need an intervention, and the other half trying to get a stimming child to stay in bed so we can attempt to actually go to sleep." Those choices in how I speak sit on top of what our nights really look like.

And that's how I balance the weight, half humour, all truths.

Because truth is, sometimes the stimming lasts for hours in the night, not just physical but vocal. Whole streams of babbling that build like an argument: pacing, flapping, tone rising and falling, as if he's in a full-blown debate with himself or with you. Other than at 3am, he'll do it most with my sister, *'Aunty Get Down'*; her anxiety is not as entertained by the *'amazing dangerousness'* as others are. Each time she yells, 'Get Down!', there is a recall and a flap, not a happy one. Rigid arms, heavier feet, and a meeting of eyebrows. Watching him, it's like seeing a heated discussion in a foreign tongue: rhythm, passion, release.

7. *Translucent Need:* **Stimming and Repetitive Behaviours**
8. *Translucent Need:* **Vocal Stimming**

And in our family, it isn't brushed off as nonsense; it's entertainment. He times his babbles like punchlines, trading volleys with my sister as if he's a little old man on a tirade. The cousins double over laughing, convinced he's cussing her out in some secret toddler dialect. In their eyes, it isn't just noise. It's personality, mischief, defiance, and it lands like language.

In the family, it's comedy; in nursery, it's data.

So, to staff, my tone comes with more caution: "He slept well last night, but I have noticed that his nap times at home are much later than you report him going to sleep here. As I said previously, he is really Houdini and has probably figured that if he can't escape the room physically, sleep is the mental escape."

9. *Translucent Need:* **Sleep-Avoidance & Regression**

As for the teachers and staff, the empath in me knows the majority have good intentions, but where I'm from, we're also scared of Social Services, so honesty, whether in humour or plain sight, must be managed accordingly.

Because growing up Black, services were to be feared. The School, Social Services and the Police had no hierarchy. You literally thought that once they came to your home, your kids would be gone, because Black households often don't look like the adverts. And even as an adult, because my life still doesn't look like the adverts, my brain still calculates:

Mum reports two sessions in a row of sleep disruption as a cause for falling asleep in nursery = Mum can't cope or neglect + unconscious biases = "we just want to help" + Case File: HOUDINI = -Kids = RIPMe².

Because the truth is, if I answer wrong, I'm not just tired... *I'm negligent.*

Like the saying goes, there is a lot of truth said in jest, and for me, saying my truths through humour softens the stings, removes weight and the subtle giggle in response says I'm seen; And the light delivery of my problem is a subtle confirmation I am coping with it.

Not to prove anything to anyone, because the proof is in the pudding: **He's alive, isn't he?**

But when it comes to my family and friends, the empath in me worries about the fact they worry for me.

The empath in me sees their hope and expectations for him but knows that lack of acceptance plagues them. The empath in me knows that those hopeful anecdotes are not always for me; sometimes, they themselves are self-soothing the part of their brain that wants hope. To be honest, I find myself offering words for their reassurance, too. Because just like parents, friends and family spend your pregnancy anticipating his life and their role in it, and when the realities don't match, these anecdotes become part of their translucent needs coping mechanisms.

For outsiders, I started off having little scripts that made me sound like I knew what I was talking about, little sound bites you hear a doctor say, or things you hear on social media:

"He has some developmental delays, so he presents younger than his age."
or
"He has a lot of markers for his condition, and this particular behaviour is a possible associated trait."

These scripts gave me confidence, a sort of borrowed authority, but they never captured the real picture. They didn't tell you how his laughter explodes out of nowhere, instantly warming a room, or a sudden burst of heart-wrenching tears triggered by nothing, could break your heart more than any divorce. They didn't explain why the swing is his church and bubbles are his stars, or why the sight of a toothbrush in my hand can derail an entire morning.

Over time, I found more comfort in explaining him in my own words, grounded in observation and experience. I learned to protect my energy while keeping my child's needs visible, and started to build the confidence to defend my energy with assertion:

"I actually deal with a lot more than you can see." or
"I did a lot behind the scenes to make this possible." or
"You get to have the opinion 'he is fine' because of the work I put in that you don't see or know."

But if you listen, you still hear the odd echoes of my frustration that can be perceived as defensiveness.

The nuances in my community have added to my need for defence. There are the usual comments: *"He'll grow out of it,"* or *"Yuh fi beat him - cos if yuh spare di rod."*

Then you spare his first words being: *"Hello, is this Childline?"*

Sometimes spiritual theories get thrown at me, as if I've summoned this path with bad vibes and a short skirt.

And because I'm a minority in my area, I sometimes get the extra sting: the subtle (or not-so-subtle) idea that his needs are down to my skin pigment, my cultural practices, or my beliefs. Never mind that I'm four generations deep in Britain, not religious in the slightest, and my cultural highlights are a roast DINNER with rice 'n' peas on a Sunday, with the peas picked out.

10. *Translucent Need:* **Bias & Coping Overlap**

And maybe that's why I circle back to translucency itself. Everyone is translucent to some extent. We all carry unseen layers, quirks, defences, sensory pulls. For most people, the balance doesn't tip far enough to need a label.

But when it's your child, those layers aren't abstract. They're daily. They're lived in parks, in kitchens, in waiting rooms. And that's the difference: what someone else calls a spectrum, I call a Tuesday. It's standing in the middle of a park, explaining those layers to a stranger while trying to keep a swing in motion and a second child dangling from a frame like a stunt double rehearsing her role in *Spider-Man*.

11. *Translucent Need:* **Emotional Resilience and Empowerment**

Sometimes, I want to scream: "He doesn't need to like you, Karen, he's three years old and doesn't even respond to his own name. Bigger things going on here."

But instead, I smile, nod, and save my fight for later, for him. Because that's where it counts.

So, when I'm stood in February, swing chains burning my palms, watching bare toes turn into icebergs, I remind myself: this isn't the *Titanic*. We don't sink. We swing, we laugh, we survive, translucency and all.

Pep Talk

 Your chaos is not failure: It's proof you keep showing up. Every barefoot swing, every meltdown survived, is love in motion.

Reflection

Your child is not broken, and neither are you. Translucency is frustrating because the world rewards extremes: either visibly different or visibly typical. But your child is real, whole, and valid in the messy middle. Naming that truth gives you back power.

Next time someone says, "He looks fine," you can smile (or not) and know: "we both see different layers, but mine is the one that matters."

Translucent Needs Identified

1. **Sensory Seeking Behaviours** - *Children may reject clothing or textures and instead seek regulation through movement: swinging, climbing, spinning, or jumping. These repetitive actions help them manage overstimulation or discomfort in their bodies.*

2. **Motor Extremes** - *Strength, speed, and force often go beyond typical limits. Proprioception, awareness of the body in space, may be heightened or under-regulated, leading to fearless climbing, crashing, or testing boundaries in ways that appear superhuman.*

3. **Risk Tolerance & Thrill-Seeking** - *Drawn to high-intensity play and physical risk, they may underestimate danger while pursuing thrills. What looks reckless is often a drive for sensory input and control, making risk-taking a form of self-regulation.*

4. **Parent Sensory Load** - *Caring for a child with heightened sensory needs amplifies the caregiver's own stress. The constant noise, vigilance, and environmental triggers can overload parents' nervous systems, demanding coping strategies to remain present and safe.*

5. **Social & Communication Style** - *Instead of seeking people, they may focus on objects, repetitive play, or familiar routines. Social reciprocity: eye contact, greetings, back-and-forth play, may be limited, creating a mismatch between typical expectations and their natural style.*

6. **Parent Communication Strategies** - *To manage judgement or misunderstanding, parents often rely on humour, quick scripts, or soft deflection. These tools mask the depth of daily challenges, protecting both their child's dignity and the parent's own energy.*

7. **Stimming & Repetitive Behaviours** - *Repetitive actions such as hand-flapping, rocking, or spinning objects are not "bad habits" but essential regulation. They allow children to release emotional tension, manage sensory overload, and anchor themselves in unpredictable environments.*

8. **Vocal Stimming** - *Speech-like sounds, babbling, or repeated vocal rhythms provide the same regulation as physical stims. To outsiders it may sound like nonsense, defiance or even speech, but it is expression in its truest form, communication through sound, cadence, and energy.*

9. **Sleep-Avoidance & Regression** - *Sleep can shift in two directions. Some children use it as a retreat from overstimulation or social demands, while others find rest difficult because their bodies remain highly alert. Even*

with routines, baths, or weighted blankets, sleep may not come easily, and nights can stretch into unsociable hours for everyone caring for them.

10. **Bias & Coping Overlap** - *On top of navigating complex needs, families may face cultural or social stereotypes. Well-meaning advice or harmful assumptions layer onto the parenting load, forcing parents to defend not only their child's needs but also their identity and culture.*

11. **Emotional Resilience & Empowerment** - *Parents of translucent children must hold confidence in their child's worth, even when the world questions it. Advocacy becomes empowerment, affirming their child's validity while finding strength in vulnerability.*

CHAPTER 2

SILENT HOUDINI

"When I vanish, I'm not gone; I'm finding the next door."

Chapter 2
Silent Houdini

If Chapter 1 was about surviving the park with strangers watching, Chapter 2 is about surviving my own house with *no one* watching, and honestly, that's worse.

Because my child? He is Silent Houdini.

You can blink, and he has vanished. One second, he's humming by the window, the next he's scaling kitchen counters with the speed of a ninja cat. You don't hear footsteps, or crashes, or the usual thud-thud-thud of a toddler testing gravity. So, silence in my house is not peace; it's a threat.

Enter the Queen's Guards: my eldest son and my daughter, drafted without choice into the household's prison guard service. Their role? Surveillance. Their weapons? Sharp eyes, loud voices, and the constant call-and-response that echoes through my home.

"Is he with you?"
"No, I thought he was with *you!*"
"So where is he then?"
"I've found him!"

It happens every few minutes. If the house goes too quiet, the alarm sounds. The Guards go searching. Because when Houdini vanishes, he doesn't leave breadcrumbs; he leaves chaos.

A bedroom door left open? Pillows pulled off the bed, desk accessories scattered as if a tornado had passed through.
The kitchen? Chairs dragged to the counter, every cupboard door ajar.

The staircase? Don't even get me started. The boy has Velcro in his hands and feet, I swear he could climb a wall if he fancied it. Windowsill, cupboard top, bookcase? No problem. And because he's not stupid, he stacks objects into stepladders like some kind of toddler engineer.

This is his *Danger Perception:* not recognising risk, only recognising opportunity.

He's also a connoisseur of textures. If it feels different, he tests it.

And his greatest love? Water.
Not just in cups. Not just in baths. Everywhere. He will spit water onto surfaces just to watch how it pools and runs, how it changes under light. To him, it's science. To me, it's another mop-and-bucket workout I never signed up for.

But the bath may be the only place water isn't favourable. Ever since a wash-hair day eighteen months ago, he refuses to sit down in the tub naked. But let my back be turned on an empty bath and he's fully dressed, and suddenly his love of water and the bathtub connect. He plays the lead of his own movie: *Aquaman: The Toddler Years.*

And now…his latest discovery, nappies. The textures inside. Let's just say it's silent play… until the smell gets loud enough to summon the Guards.

That's when my daughter bursts in, nose wrinkled, waving her arms like she's directing traffic:
"Muuuuum! He's at it again!"
The Queen's Guards, trained by experience, always arrive when the air quality shifts.

12. Translucent Need: **Digestive and Environmental Impact**

Most toddlers get bored when you stop them doing something. Mine? He gets focused. Laser-focused. You block one escape route; he will test the same spot fifty-six times in a row, with the patience of a saint and the persistence of a debt collector.

This is his *Hyperfocus Persistence:* not determination as choice, but compulsion dressed as brilliance.

You move the furniture? He moves his tactics. You lock the door? He studies the hinges. By bedtime, you're not just parenting; you're living inside a live-action version of *Prison Break.*

And here's the kicker: it's not just funny stories for the group chat. It's bruises, burns, and near heart attacks.

Like the time he climbed onto the cooker and burned himself, third-degree. And he didn't cry. Not once. I only noticed hours later when I changed him for bed. Imagine explaining that to the hospital:

"Yes, he climbed on the cooker. Yes, he got third-degree burns. No, he didn't cry. Yes, I was home. No, I'm not making this up."

13. *Translucent Need:* **High Pain Threshold**

That's not a parenting anecdote. That's a Social Services case waiting to happen.

And then came *The Great Escape.*
The carpets were being professionally cleaned because, let's face it, some of these online hacks aren't hacking. Furniture was crammed upstairs or piled in the dining area. Chaos. But for Houdini? Mum had turned into God and created heaven: a high-risk, end-your-life, indoor obstacle course.

Whilst I tried to keep my sanity, I requested the Guards keep Houdini in the lower cells while I prepped the upper quadrants. During this time, my female guard, trying to fulfil her second duty as maid, had taken out the recycling. She came back in and shut the door, assuming Houdini was with the other guard. He, in turn, assumed Houdini was upstairs with me.

It wasn't until a knock at the door that anyone realised the disappearing act. A stranger asked if we owned a Houdini, because he was currently a quarter-mile up the road, barefoot, no nappy with a snotty nose.

In two odd slippers, a Macy Gray-style afro, and my homeless-looking, bleached-stained house-tracksuit; I ran like my life depended on it. At a quick glance, I could have easily passed for a 15-year-old drill rapper.

When I reached the church, there he was, naked, snotty-nosed, with two Police officers and a lady by the squad car, plus what looked like the entire village spectating.

And let me say this. That day, being the only Black face in the village was my blessing. Because how else would anyone have identified a non-speaking, naked toddler a quarter-mile from home? He could have been just another child gone wandering, but no. He was clearly mine.

My difference that day was his safety net… But possibly not mine.

The shorter officer was holding Houdini by the cuff of his t-shirt, the other standing nearby, keeping the crowd calm. A lady leaned against the squad car, clipboard in hand, looked me up and down as if I owed her rent money.

This is it, I thought to myself. They've seen *Top Boy*. To them, I might as well be Jacq. They're taking my baby. My name is going on a poster at the next BLM march, because let me tell you, I'd go Scarface-style for my kids, hurling nappies instead of bullets: *"Say hello to my little friends."*

But instead of being cuffed and body-slammed against the squad car, the shorter officer just looked… human.

He offered me a lift back to the house. Once inside, the three threaded through the obstacle course, saw food in the fridge and cupboards. And then, the same officer who had been clasping Houdini at the scene, said the words I'll never forget:

"I have a family too. This seems like a lot. But you also seem in control. Mistakes happen. He's safe."

For once, someone stared long enough. They saw the translucency.

14. *Translucent Need: **Elopement Risk***

After that day, I wasn't taking chances.

Cue the Amazon security haul. Door locks and cupboard bolts. Baby gates? Please. For Houdini they're hurdles. For me, a yo-yo of three, up and down the stairs every five minutes, they were a *Crystal Maze* challenge I didn't need.

Now, the internal doors lock from the outside, limiting his access to different "cells." The guards can now stay in their watching towers and maintain an increased level of surveillance.

And still, Houdini finds a way.

Case in point: one day the silence was too loud for our house. The call went up: "Is he with you?" All responses: no. Panic. Quick scan of his usual spots. Nothing.

This time, a little better dressed, but hair still undone, I bolted down the road, screaming his name as if I expected a response, the middle guard at my heels… only to get a call from the senior guard saying he could hear heavy breathing near the back door.

When he pulled back the hood of the pram, there was Houdini, sitting in silence, munching on an antique biscuit. New hiding place noted. Everyday Houdini moment logged.

Real Talk

Some parents panic at the first cry. I panic at the silence.

Pep Talk

 If your child is also a Silent Houdini, let me give you this pep talk:

- You are not paranoid. You are adapting.

- Your house looks like Fort Knox because it needs to.

- Other people might think you're over the top. Let them. They don't know what it's like to live with a child who can unlock the front door before he can say his own name.

And remember: Houdini may be silent, but you are not alone.

Reflection

That day stuck with me more than most. Not because Houdini escaped, that's his trademark, but because of what it showed me about my other children. My Queen's Guards aren't just kids anymore: they're guards, reporters, backup alarms. And that vigilance, that constant watch, it comes at a cost.

Childhood should be freedom, but in my house, it doubles as surveillance duty. They've learned that silence can scream danger. They've learned to call for me like they're manning radio towers in wartime. And while I'm grateful, deeply grateful, I also feel the sting of guilt, because their childhood comes second to his safety.

And maybe that's the part people don't see. What feels like exposure can sometimes be protection. That day in the village, my difference marked him safe, even if it could have marked me at risk. In our house, their vigilance does the same. Safety for him always carries a cost for someone else.

And that truth demands I honour their sacrifices every single day. There isn't a second adult in the house to share the load, no one to swap shifts with, no fallback when my energy drains. So, the Guards step up, too often, too soon. And that's not just resilience, it's sacrifice. I honour it out loud, today.

Translucent Needs Identified

12. **Digestive and Environmental Impact** - *Restricted diets from sensory avoidance can create internal imbalances that show up in the most practical of ways, stools with extreme odours. The smell permeates the home, requiring external waste bins, constant ventilation, and adjustments that affect the whole family's daily environment.*

13. **High Pain Threshold** - *Injuries, discomfort, or illness may not be expressed in typical ways. Children may continue playing, climbing, or running despite burns, cuts, or fevers, making vigilance more critical for caregivers.*

14. **Elopement Risk** - *A tendency to bolt, wander, or escape from safe areas without awareness of danger. Requires constant supervision and often transforms everyday spaces into high-risk environments.*

CHAPTER 3

THE PAPERWORK PRISON

"Tick the squares if you must. I
live between the lines."

Chapter 3
The Paperwork Prison

If my son is Silent Houdini at home, then outside, I'm the prisoner.
My jailer? Paperwork. Forms so long they could double as
wallpaper, questions so cold they could make you forget your own
child's name.

Every new service, every new referral, every new "support" comes
with another pack of papers. Half the time, I wonder if Houdini
could scale the stack like one of his climbing towers and finally
touch the ceiling he's been aiming for.

It's relentless. By the time you finish one form, another drops
through the letterbox, like the system's signed up to *Amazon Prime*
for paperwork.

This is where reality and reports stop speaking the same language.

I say:
"He paces back and forth for hours, loves bubbles, and won't wear socks."
They write:
"Displays sensory-seeking repetitive behaviours with tactile
resistance."

I say:
"He escapes like Houdini, blink, and he's gone."
They write:
"Demonstrates elopement behaviours requiring environmental
safety considerations."

15. *Translucent Need: **The Language Barrier***

And in the translation, something precious gets lost. The fire, the humour, the humanity. My child becomes bullet points on a form, stripped of personality, reduced to symptoms.

The system positions itself like a caregiver, but the reality? It's another child on my to-do list. Endless calls, appointments, chasing letters, waiting lists.

It's wild. My son tests physical locks; the system tests my stamina. One scales cupboards while the other piles acronyms: SALT *(Speech and Language Therapy)*, EHCP, CAMHS: a whole alphabet of hoops to jump through. And if you don't know what half of those mean, congratulations … you're free. I had to learn them by force.

Sometimes I think if I ever wrote my real job title, it would be: *Full-Time Parent. Part-Time Prison Warden. Accidental Case Manager.* And that's me with qualifications, a good laptop, and a stubborn streak; what about the parents who don't have the words, the time, or the fight?

And you know what? None of this admin puts food in the fridge, none of it keeps him safe, and none of it replaces my actual presence as his mother.

When I first contemplated doing the DLA form, it asked me to get evidence from a professional. Being on every waiting list means there are none outside of nursery. The form mentioned that inclusion of an ILP *(Individual Learning Plan)* could support the application.

So, I immediately contacted his nursery. Along with the ABC, LMNOP and the other acronyms they'd thrown at me, I was sure I'd heard them mention doing an ILP for him. They were very willing to assist and said I could collect it at the next session.

When I arrived, his key worker handed me an envelope and said these were the documents I had requested with the addition of his attendance record and a report with details collected from his burn injury and *Great Escape.*

I thought: *Great. Finally, a little something that's going to make this DLA form the size of the Yellow Pages worth sending.*

I had three hours before he needed to be collected, so thought, home – library – post office – pick-up. But when I got home, sat at the kitchen side where the DLA form mountain waited, I opened the envelope.

And honestly? I thought maybe they'd accidentally given me the wrong child's file, or it was another child's messy play. Because there is no way that this was written by an advanced 3-year-old, let alone a trained paid professional.

Once I deciphered the Morse code, it listed exactly two actions:
- *"Climb less."*
- *"Play with a toy."*

And under *"How will this be measured?"* they'd written:
- **"Less climbing."**
- **"Playing with a toy."**

Pause: *What in the actual fudge was this?*

This wasn't strategy. This wasn't even language. No tools, no interventions, no safeguarding value; just a three-month review to "fix" something that wasn't broken, while ignoring the real needs.

It was like asking a fish to practice swimming.

And this is the danger with these tick-box targets, they don't even reflect how he plays. They likely sat him in front of flashing-light toys and noisy gadgets, waiting for a reaction. But those overwhelm him.

What he seeks is cause-and-effect: push, pull, press, repeat. And here's the thing; he doesn't want to be guided through it, he wants to guide *you*. He'll drag your hand onto the button and flap with joy when you press, but if you try to shape his hand, he'll pull away and reset the play on his own terms.

None of that fits neatly on a line that says "play with a toy." It's not absence of play. It's mismatch of measure.

And here's the kicker: I'd already written on the DLA form that he *does* play with toys. So, if I send this, one of us is lying. If the ILP had picked up on those details, it might have looked like understanding. Instead, it read like guesswork.

16. Translucent Need: **Measurement Mismatch**

Not every professional missed it, though. One health visitor actually listened. She didn't just tick boxes in an office; she came to my home, sat in my living room, and watched him perform all his chaos: eating draft excluders, scaling the TV unit, hanging upside down to watch cartoons. She saw what I saw. She knew this wasn't just "toddler energy," and even though he was below the guideline age for referral, she pushed it through almost a year early. That's the difference when the measure matches the reality: you get truth instead of guesswork.

And later that afternoon, Silent Houdini chose to demonstrate his cause-and-effect, by joining in the admin game.

As I sat there clutching the so-called "ILP," contemplating what to do, Houdini swooped like a magpie, grabbed the page in his death grip, and clenched it as if he expected juice to pour out. By the time I prised it from his fingers, it had torn, right across the one piece of "evidence" I had from a "professional" to support his claim.

Which only proved what I already knew: if the paperwork couldn't survive a toddler's grip, it was never strong enough to hold his truth.

Then came the nursery's *24-month developmental assessment.* According to this report, Houdini: couldn't drink from a cup, and couldn't stay awake longer than two hours. But he could do all those things. Which left me thinking either they weren't really observing him, or outside of my care he was so undermet that his coping mechanisms were simply to stim and sleep.

And that's the danger. If they see him as worse than he is, he won't get the right support for his level, and then he really will fall further behind.

We waited nine months for the speech and language assessment. Nine. Months. When we finally went, Houdini threatened the employment of every staff member in the waiting area.

If a door could be pushed, he went through it. A chair? Climbed. The water dispenser? Tipped. Windows and glass doors? Licked. All this, barefoot, in a dirty NHS waiting room. By the time we were called, I'd lost the will to live. Forty-eight minutes of hurdling chairs, blocking exits, and shielding strangers from a toddler streaking past. The pram was wedged against the only door, so I played guard while Sheila and Edna compared Tenerife to Majorca, until Sheila pivoted, mid-glance at me, towards Nigeria. Apparently, she visited there eight years ago: as if that somehow made us kin.

It's the same way people hear "Jamaican" and think they're safe if they drop *"Wah Gwan"* or jerk chicken into the chat. As if being Black anywhere is one universal experience. Within five minutes, we were back in the waiting area. Houdini half-undressed, me wrestling with his jacket zip, and Edna's knee one collision away from permanent retirement.

The consultation had consisted of Houdini scaling her desk while she called his name, then turning to me and saying:
"You're right, he doesn't respond to his name."
No shit, Sherlock.

17. *Translucent Need:* **Limited Social Reciprocity**

She asked a few more questions about words and needs, then told me we'd now been referred to speech and language, with a waiting list of around two years.

Wait… hang on. I thought we were seeing *speech and language* today. As in, the service we waited nine months for.

Apparently not. But she didn't forget to hand me a stack of leaflets that could probably keep me busy reading for those two years while we waited.

Real Talk

The paperwork doesn't just take time; it takes pieces of me. Every form I fill feels like carving Houdini down into boxes he doesn't fit in. Every acronym feels like another wall between us and the help he actually needs.

Some days it feels less like applying for support and more like begging for permission to mother my own son. And that's the part they'll never put in a report: the system doesn't just test your child; it tests you, over and over, until you start to wonder if survival itself counts as evidence.

Pep Talk

If you're knee-deep in forms, waiting lists, and endless acronyms, hear this:

- You are **not** failing. The system is failing to see your child clearly.

- Your handwriting doesn't have to look like a professional's. Your lived words matter.

- Evidence can be shredded, reports can be wrong, but your daily reality is undeniable.

The forms may define your child in bullet points, but **you** live the full paragraphs. And that's what counts.

Reflection

This is the daily contradiction. The system needs me to be fluent in their language, their acronyms, their metrics. And I can do that; I recognise the privilege of being able to articulate, sometimes better than the professionals themselves.

But it leaves me wondering: what about the parents who can't? Parents with their own translucent needs, who can't fathom these forms, let alone deliver the "evidence"?

How many children get lost in translation; not because their needs aren't real, but because the paperwork couldn't capture them; a reminder that translation without understanding is just another form of erasure.

Translucent Needs Identified

15. **The Language Barrier** - *Parents describe lived chaos in everyday words, while professionals reduce it to clinical jargon. Important details and humanity often get lost in translation, leaving children flattened into bullet points.*

16. **Measurement Mismatch** - *Tick-box toys and targets don't always match how our kids play. When the tools miss the way they really engage, the system reads absence instead of presence, and compliance instead of truth.*

17. **Limited Social Reciprocity** - *Reduced or inconsistent responses to name, greetings, expressions, or gestures. Interaction may be selective, leaving outsiders unsure, while families learn to read subtler cues of connection.*

CHAPTER 4

THE QUEEN'S GUARDS

"They watch to keep me safe,
I play to keep us close.
That's our kind of teamwork."

Chapter 4
The Queen's Guards

Because if I am the Queen, then they, my eldest son and my daughter, are the guards. Drafted without choice, armed with nothing but watchful eyes and a loud "MUM!" on repeat, they patrol the house.

By now, the *"Is he with you?"* routine is a broken record in our home. We've rehearsed it so many times it's practically our family theme song. Only now, the calls aren't just to locate Houdini: they're checking on each other, making sure no one's cracked under pressure.

And when the house goes silent, too silent, the alarm bells start ringing. Because silence in my home doesn't mean peace. It means Houdini has vanished, and if Houdini has vanished, chaos is about to follow.

My eldest guard had dreams of one day, both of them becoming professional players, cheering each other on from the spectator's seat, as each played a cup final or lifted a trophy… sharing those moments was the vision. Football is his language, his passion, and when he found out he was getting a brother, you could see he had already carved out a pathway to the World Cup in his head.

But Houdini? He'll rip the ball down without a glance. Not to be cruel, it's just not where his eyes, hands, or heart go.

My daughter, too, had her own vision. She wanted to teach him to draw or at least appreciate the drawings she made for him. But Houdini's art gallery is in the way he flaps his hands, or how he smears water across glass.

At first, it wasn't so obvious to them. Lots of toddlers don't talk or join in certain games. But as time passes, the gap grows. The things he *doesn't* do become louder to them than the things he does.

On the rare occasion we have visitors, the questions get trickier for them.

One time, the middle guard had a friend over after school. They were sitting in the living room when Houdini bolted through, three-legged, water dripping and chewing the hair of a Barbie as if it was the most delicious snack.

Her friend's face froze. *"Why is his bum out?"* she whispered. My daughter didn't flinch. She just shrugged, reclaimed her Barbie, and said matter-of-factly, *"He's Houdini. Pants don't stay on him."* Then she carried on colouring like this was the most normal thing in the world. And maybe for her, it is. That's the thing about siblings: they become fluent in their brother's translucency. They don't always have the right words, but they have the confidence to stand in the awkward gaps and normalise what other people see as strange.

18. Translucent Need: **Sibling Adaptation**

Then there's the lampshade question. *"Why is that on the floor?"* someone once asked.

My daughter gave the same shrug, same tone: *"He's Houdini. Lampshades don't stay up with him."*

To her, it's just fact. To me, it's resilience wrapped in childhood simplicity.

Once, on a quick-sweep surveillance for Houdini, I clocked he was up in the senior guard's tower. He was on a video call to his mate when I heard the voice through the phone ask, *"How comes he won't look at the phone or say hello?"*

"Cos he doesn't like people or your big face, Bruv," was the reply, followed by a cheeky cackle. Then in the most endearing tone: *"But trust, he loves me."*

It wasn't rehearsed. It wasn't softened. Just said straight, like fact. That's what struck me: they're not only translating their brother, but they're also defending him and doing it in a way that doesn't make him smaller.

Sometimes I wonder if they wish for different. Not different, as in a world without Houdini, but the world they had before, with two parents, and a mum who wasn't in survival mode. The one who could listen to a full story without her eyes flicking between them and Houdini, making sure he wasn't halfway up a curtain pole.

Before Houdini, I was there for most things. Not everything, no parent can claim perfection, but big or small, five minutes or an hour, I showed up. Now? Sometimes it's sixty seconds of eye contact before my attention swings back to Houdini, and they feel it.

After the split, the other parent took them on their first holiday together, but Houdini didn't go. His needs were considered "a bit too much."

The house was quieter than usual that week. Too quiet for a boy who fills silence with movement.

His other parent's distance is its own kind of translucency: not loud, not dramatic, just an absence that weighs heavier than words. I've learned that fathers can carry their own translucent needs: sometimes it's denial, or the fear that the child's diagnosis says something about them. It could be fear that they'll be judged through the child's diagnosis or pride that makes hands-off feel safer than hands-on.

It doesn't make the load lighter for me, but it provides a soft explanation to some of the cracks the guards notice; the ones that make them wonder why their home doesn't have two parents, the way every child instinctively expects.

19. Translucent Need: **Male Presence and Denial**

My daughter asked if Houdini was the reason he no longer lived here. I reassured her it wasn't, but the fact she even asked shows me they see the patterns. They notice the weight. They feel the difference.

But here's the truth: if Houdini isn't around, he's the first to be missed. And luckily for all of us, he's the only baby brother they've ever had. They don't compare him because they've never had another to measure against.

And there are men who show up: uncles, granddads, step-dads, friends: quiet, steady, hands-on. They don't trend. They build.

My eldest is more than just a brother, but I'll never make him a substitute dad. That's not his role, and I guard against piling my load onto him. Still, expectations sit on his shoulders. What he gives his brother is something I can't replicate: a masculine energy.

Most of the professionals around Houdini are women: teachers, therapists, healthcare staff, so his time with men is limited. And yet, with his brother, you see subtle differences: the way Houdini responds to his deeper voice, the way he follows his movements, sometimes more than he does with me. It's not about better or worse, simply different, and in our world, those differences matter.

But all my kids have translucent needs I recognise. A teenager, no matter who they are, is translucent in needs and emotions: puberty is not for the faint.

My daughter, the only girl, is learning womanhood not from the gentle lessons I longed to give, but from watching me survive. In our kingdom, she sees me reach for armour before silk, steel before softness. She deserved nurture before necessity, yet she's learning that sometimes the crown is heavy, and the shield comes first. And so, her lesson in womanhood is forged not only in tenderness, but in resilience.

And me, a single parent, carrying the weight of discerning whose "translucent needs" get priority when, in our world at home, only Houdini's are "transparent."

And yet, I can't carry all of this alone.

That's where family steps in, not just for Houdini, but for the Guards. They'll take him for a day so I can take them out solo: cinema, a football game, even just a walk without scanning the horizon for escapes. Those one-to-one moments matter. They remind the Guards they are more than watchmen; they are children, worthy of undivided attention.

Like the time I took my daughter to our first 4DX cinema experience. I wanted her to have the best, so I even asked ChatGPT for seat recommendations. She hates water, I get motion sickness, and still we ended up sprayed and spun like a *rinse and spin* cycle.

But we laughed through every second.

Or the celebrity football match with my son. I thought seeing Will Smith was the win, but no, it was a group of scruffy YouTubers with a packet of sweets. One photo later and I'd earned the title: "Your mum's a legend."

That's all I needed to hear.

These moments are more than just outings; they're reminders that the Guards deserve joy on their own terms too.

Holidays, too, are a village effort. A waterpark would be impossible alone. But with cousins, siblings, aunties, and uncles, the load spreads and the laughter multiplies. The Guards get to play, I get to breathe, and Houdini? He still finds ways to headline the show.

Because it's not just me or the Guards. The wider family get pulled into Houdini's orbit too. On holidays, when the load is shared, the cousins become junior Guards without even realising it, but they don't complain. To them, he isn't just chaos, he's charisma.

If an uncle scores a tiny win, like throwing him in the air at just the right angle, Houdini will demand it again and again until the uncle is begging for mercy. His cousins watch, wide-eyed, whispering, *"Baby Houdini is so cool, I wanna do that."* They don't just guard him, they admire him.

And yet, no matter how many cousins join the watch, no matter how many uncles get drafted in for the tiny wins, the truth remains: my Guards are still children first. Their laughter, their school runs, their silly stories deserve as much space as Houdini's chaos.

So, I carry the weight, I share it when I can, but I never forget... my job isn't just to keep them guarding. It's to keep them growing.

 Real Talk

Statistically, parents of children with additional needs are more likely to separate or divorce than the general population. But that's not my story.

My story? Oh, we're not ready for that, not here anyway. I'd probably end up in a lawsuit with Tyler Perry because he'd instantly be inspired. Just tell him to cast Taraji P. Henson to play me, and let's call it a day.

Pep Talk

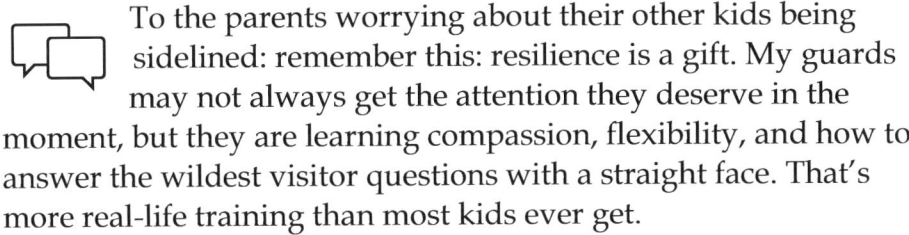

To the parents worrying about their other kids being sidelined: remember this: resilience is a gift. My guards may not always get the attention they deserve in the moment, but they are learning compassion, flexibility, and how to answer the wildest visitor questions with a straight face. That's more real-life training than most kids ever get.

And to the siblings themselves: you are not forgotten. You are seen, you are needed, and your role is more powerful than you realise. One day, you'll look back and see that your love held the walls up when everything else felt shaky.

Reflection

The truth is resilience has a price tag. My eldest two aren't just children; they're Guards drafted into duty too soon. They love their brother without hesitation, but love doesn't erase the weight of responsibility. Childhood should be a playground, not a watchtower, but in our house, it's both.

And with no weekends, half-terms, or holiday splits, there are no natural breaks. Sometimes it falls to friends, family, or even the wider community to step into roles they were never meant to fill, just to give the Guards a night off, to remind them they're children too. That's the cost of the missing parent: others carrying weight that was never theirs.

20. Translucent Need: **Absent-Parent Load**

But here's the balance: every sacrifice chisels something into them. Compassion. Wit. A fluency in love that doesn't need words. They already know how to stand tall in awkward gaps, how to defend someone without shrinking them, how to hold chaos and tenderness in the same breath.

So yes, their childhood carries an extra weight. But my job now is to make sure it also carries joy. To guard not just Houdini's safety, but their right to laughter, silliness, and freedom. Because beyond their titles as Guards, they're still just kids, and their childhood deserves protecting as fiercely as Houdini's magic.

Their resilience is their inheritance, but joy must be their legacy.

Translucent Needs Identified

18. **Sibling Adaptation** - *Siblings normalise their brother or sister's differences from an early age. They explain behaviours to peers, carry responsibilities quietly, and often sacrifice pieces of their own childhood.*

19. **Male Presence and Denial** - *Fathers and male carers may experience their own translucent needs, often unseen. Denial, minimising behaviours, or emotional withdrawal can stem from fear, shame, or cultural expectations around masculinity. This isn't always physical absence; sometimes they are present in body but absent in acknowledgement of the child's reality. The strain falls on relationships as much as on caregiving.*

20. **Absent-Parent Load** - *When one parent isn't physically present or sharing care, the weight doesn't disappear; it redistributes. Siblings, grandparents, and the wider community quietly absorb responsibilities that shouldn't fall on them, reshaping childhoods and households in ways that linger long after the moment.*

CHAPTER 5

TINY WINS AND TOASTED ART

"You call it chaos, I call it creating. Even the toaster wanted to feel alive."

Chapter 5
Tiny Wins and Toasted Art

Parenting Houdini is a full-body workout in crisis management. But every now and then, in the middle of the madness, he gifts me something so absurd, so unexpected, that I can't help but laugh. These are the tiny wins. The moments that break the heaviness, the "if you don't laugh, you'll cry" reminders that humour really is survival.

Now, most people replace a toaster once every few years. In my house? We're on toaster number three this year, and honestly, I've stopped calling it an appliance. It's an art installation.

Because when Houdini melted it into a Salvador Dalí inspired sculpture, all I could think was there is probably some eccentric art collector out there who would pay thousands for this. I could've listed it as:
"Untitled No. 3 (Childhood Chaos in Plastic). Starting bid: £2,500."

Instead, it went in the bin. But that's translucent parenting in a nutshell: what looks like destruction to the world, looks like creation when you tilt your head and squint.

If you think mealtimes are about nutrition, think again. In our house, it's WWE. Houdini (**The Undertaker**) vs. Mum (**Stone Cold Steve Austin**).

If it isn't Wotsits or chicken dippers, it's a plate of food groups served Stone Cold Stunner style. Houdini bolts at the sight of a plate and spoon: full 100-metre dash. He'll smash into walls or doorframes trying to escape.

If I catch him (and that's a big if), it's a bear hug pin-down while I prise open his mouth. If the flavour or texture isn't right? Straight pellet to my face.

Score: Undertaker 1–0 Stone Cold

If he likes it? He chews, I release, and suddenly the Royal Rumble is over.

Score: Undertaker 1–1 Stone Cold

Then, like nothing happened, he casually strolls over, mouth wide open, demanding the spoon. And God forbid I don't move quick enough.

Final Score: Stone Cold by TKO.

21. *Translucent Need: **Food Aversion due to Sensory Processing***

Then there was the day I upgraded the pram. Houdini had been escaping the old one, so I thought: new model, tighter straps, job done. Rookie mistake.

I left him strapped in on the front step while I carried shopping into the kitchen. The distance from the front door to the kitchen is 3.5 metres, the same hallway I once measured for a runner after the carpet-cleaning chaos of The Great Escape. Seven strides, two carrier bags on the counter, I turn around… and the pram is empty.

These straps were supposed to be harder to get out of. But what was I even thinking? This is Houdini I'm dealing with.
I look out: garden path, street, no sign of a sprinting silhouette. I'm ready to run when I hear his grunt. There he is, perched on the sofa, remote in hand like he's been waiting all day for me to switch the TV on.

Tiny win: I learnt in the safest way possible that no pram, no strap, no upgrade will ever outwit Houdini.

Now, I don't know if I'm showing my age, but as a kid we often played *Blind Man's Bluff*. No offence intended but we just weren't very PC in the 90s. We weren't very sensitive to names or safety either. But as kids we loved it.

Reflecting now, it was basically a hospital trip waiting to happen: a blindfolded kid in a cluttered box bedroom with bunkbeds, a wardrobe and drawers, fumbling around in the dark trying to grab five or six kids leaping from danger to danger. I'm fairly sure no parent ever approved this. But that's Houdini's favourite game at bedtime. Climbing from danger to danger in the dark, and the blindfolded kid trying to grab? Me.

Why not switch the light on? Because light stimulates his senses, and that means two more hours awake. On the odd occasion I do flick the switch, it's like the *"hit the switch challenge."* I'm convinced I hear him at the end of the bed, but when the light comes on, he's perched on the windowsill, squinting from light overload, grinning like the Cheshire Cat from Alice in Wonderland.

Another thing Houdini has taught me: a lot of retailers are lying. Blackout blinds? *My backside.* Let my neighbour pull up with her headlights on and the car might as well be in the room. That tiny trickle of light that seeps through. For Houdini, it's sunrise.

Then there are the rare nights when Houdini behaves like a guard. A bowl of Weetabix with no Royal Rumble. A warm bath. And then, semi-wrapped in a towel, lotion massaging into his skin, the telltale signs appear: the roll back of the eyes, the slower breathing, the heavy drop of his leg.

And I think: tonight, I might put on a face mask, I might scroll online, or I might just have the ultimate reward: a sleep of more than four hours.

That's not a tiny win. That's a gold, first-place podium victory moment for the Queen herself.

Then there are his laughs. Not the ticklish giggles he gives when you stroke his thigh during a nappy change, as foul as those nappies smell, they're daily highlights too. I'm talking about the deep, belly laughs that arrive out of nowhere, unsolicited.

He'll be in the living room, the guards and the Queen off in their own corners of the palace, when suddenly the walls shake with his joy. And in those moments, the bolts on the doors don't feel like prison locks anymore, they feel like the gates to his kingdom. Because the second that laugh erupts, every guard abandons their post to see what's set him off, as if he were watching a personal episode of You've Been Framed.

And only Houdini and God know what the joke is. But it happens often. And every time, it feels like his version of a tiny win.

Not all tiny wins are mine. Sometimes they belong to the guards. Like the rare moment when the senior guard is convinced he hears Houdini mimicking a sound, maybe even trying to form a word. Instantly, the whole house crowds round like it's the EastEnders Christmas special. We hold our breath. We dare to believe.

Or the times when middle guard somehow gets him wrapped up in a blanket on the sofa, lying still, both glued to nursery rhymes on YouTube. How she convinces him to stay put that long is beyond me. It's sorcery.

Tiny win: the guards get proof that their brother does connect, in his own way.

Here's the thing: tiny wins aren't always big achievements. They're the sanity points that keep the game going:

- **1 point** for making it through the supermarket without Houdini scaling the shelves.
- **5 points** if the guards actually finish their chips before resuming surveillance.

- **10 points** if nothing ends up broken, flooded, or melted into "art."

- **20 bonus points** if Houdini seals your efforts with his signature flap and bounce of approval.

That's how we win. Not in the glossy, Instagrammable way. But in the "we survived today and laughed once" way.

Real Talk

Tiny wins aren't cute, they're currency. They're the only thing between me and collapse some days. I don't stack them in a scrapbook; I stack them like rent money, proof I've got enough to keep going.

Because under the laughs, there's the truth: if I don't count the chaos as wins, it just feels like loss. And translucent parenting doesn't give you the luxury of waiting for milestones. You take what you get: melted toasters, four hours of sleep, a laugh that shakes the walls, and you call it victory.

Pep Talk

So, here's your reminder: celebrate the tiny wins. Don't wait for the big ones to feel proud.

Did your child eat something outside their usual two foods? That's a win.
Did you catch them before they bolted into the road? That's a win.
Did you laugh? Even once, today? That's a win.

Write them down. Stack them up. Because tiny wins are the evidence that you're not just surviving translucent parenting: you're living it, one absurd, exhausting, hilarious victory at a time.

Reflection

Sometimes it feels like the world measures progress in milestones: words spoken, skills mastered, neat little checklists. But in our house? Progress is counted in tiny wins. The ones only we notice. The ones that keep us moving forward.

Tiny wins don't make the reports. They don't get written in ILPs or assessed at appointments. But they are the glue that holds the hard days together.

The system measures milestones, but I measure survival... and joy! And that's how we win.

Translucent Needs Identified

21. **Food Aversion due to Sensory Processing** - *Textures, smells, or flavours can trigger fight-or-flight reactions at mealtimes. Eating becomes a sensory battle, with stress spilling into the household and nutrition often taking a backseat to survival.*

CHAPTER 6

OUTSIDE THE GATES

"I don't need words to explain
my light.
You'll see it when you slow
down."

Chapter 6
Outside the Gates

Inside my house, Houdini is a king. He swings from his throne, rules over chaos, and commands the attention of his guards. But the second we step outside? The world stops seeing a boy and starts seeing a problem.

The stares, the side-eyes, the whispered questions: they follow us like shadows. If he bolts barefoot in February, people don't see Houdini. They see me. They see what they think is neglect, or failure, or fuss.

22. *Translucent Need: **Social Perception Load***

And that's the part that stings. Not just the judgement, but the constant sense that I must perform, to explain, excuse, or advocate, when all I really want is to be.

Here's the truth: I don't want to be an advocate or a spokeswoman. Not every day. Not at every turn. I don't need the entire world bent out of shape to fit him, especially when those bends might not even fit the guards and their translucencies. They live here too.

Houdini is not an anomaly, but his needs are not the needs of the majority. He doesn't require a separate bathroom, a new set of pronouns, or ramps installed at every turn. What he needs is much simpler: for the world to recognise that he exists.

And as cruel as the world can be, I've learned that compassion runs deeper. Most people don't need a campaign to act decent. They just need to notice the cracks of light shining through.

In Tesco, when he had shredded the bags before I'd even paid. I braced myself for the sighs, the rolling eyes. Instead, the cashier slipped me a couple more bags and said quietly, 'Don't worry, love, I've seen worse.' In that tiny gesture, the chaos felt lighter. Compassion can be as small as a free 30p carrier bag, but in that moment, it was priceless.

Or the man at the bus stop who quietly stood in front of the kerb, acting like a human barrier while Houdini wriggled in my arms, desperate to bolt.

And then there was the drunk guy on the train. Houdini was sat on my lap, doing his thing: crushing Wotsits one by one before eating them, like a crisp scientist running experiments. The man, beer can in hand, turned to me and slurred, "What's he got wrong with him? Impressive though, the way he crushed the shit out of them crisps." Then he went straight back to his lager, like nothing had happened. Small mercies move mountains on hard days.

It wasn't polished. It wasn't PC. But it was oddly endearing, because sometimes acknowledgement, even messy, feels better than silence.

These people didn't know him. But they saw him. And in that tiny shift, choosing kindness over judgement, the world bent, just enough.

That's what I ask for. Not a revolution. Not a system overhaul. Just for people to pause long enough to see him as more than his chaos.

23. *Translucent Need: **The Right to Exist Without Explanation***

Sometimes it happens in ways I never expect.

The Uber driver who asked if I wanted him to put the radio on static to soothe Houdini, instead of huffing while he kicked the seat.

The nail salon tech who, when Houdini ran laps around the salon, didn't roll her eyes but simply handed him a nail file like it was all part of the service.

The elderly lady in the post office who winked at me after Houdini flattened a display of envelopes and whispered, *"Don't worry, love, that's how geniuses start."*

None of these people joined a campaign or went through training. They just spotted the translucency, the little rays that leak out, and adapted. That's the world I want him to grow up in. Not perfect, just decent.

Take the jungle gym. Houdini could sit at the fire truck wheel for an hour, spinning like it's his life's mission. But every minute he sits there is a minute another kid doesn't get their turn.

I've been that parent too, standing there with my guard, serving up the same tired lines about patience and fairness while she waits 'unfairly' for her chance to steer. As if answering that question wasn't enough overstimulation, let alone doing it in a jungle gym.

That's the scale: it tips, it balances, and it reminds me: translucent needs don't cancel each other out. They coexist.

And then there are the *"maybe you should try…"* people. The ones who suggest weighted blankets, sugar-free diets, essential oils, or the latest parenting hack. What they don't see is the weight behind the eyes. That sometimes the suggestion they think is helpful lands like an accusation, as if I haven't already spent the night Googling, pleading, trying.

That's the part that sticks, not the words themselves, but the reminder that I am always two steps behind someone else's idea of "enough".

And the truth? Some days, even kindness feels heavy. It clings, like wet clothes, dragging me down with the reminder that I should be doing more, knowing more, being more. And in those moments, I don't want another tip; I just want to be enough as I am.

But here's the nuance: sometimes the advice hits right. A mum who leans in and says, "Hide the veg in the mash, love." A dad at the pool who whispers a travel hack that saves me three hours of meltdowns. A friend who pings me supermarket alerts when Wotsits or dippers are on offer, because she knows that's survival in bulk. And then there are the days when someone shares a video of a non-verbal kid speaking at twenty-one, and it lands like hope instead of homework.

I can't predict which days I'll cry or roll my eyes, and that's the truth: if I don't know, neither will you. So compassion, not cleverness, is what keeps the scales balanced. Advice with judgement weighs heavy. Advice with love? Sometimes it saves me.

Real Talk

I don't want to spend my life campaigning. I don't want to stand at podiums with leaflets or hashtags. And I don't need the world redrawn at every corner just to make room for him.

Real talk? Some days I want to shout his story to the rooftops; other days I just want to buy bread in Tesco without becoming a case study. Advocacy is not my life purpose. My purpose is him.

Pep Talk

To every parent who feels pressured to become the loudest advocate in the room: hear this: you don't owe the world a TED Talk on your child. You don't have to explain every meltdown, every quirk, every choice.

You also don't have to try every "maybe you should" that comes your way. Weighted blankets, diets, therapies… some will help, some won't. None of them are proof you're failing.
Because your child's existence is not a petition. It's a presence. And presence alone is powerful.

So, the next time the world stares? Stare back. You don't owe them a press release, just your child, living.

And if the world can't handle a meltdown in Tesco? Tell them to take it up with Customer Services.

Reflection

There's a fine line between advocacy and exhaustion. Between educating everyone and just surviving the day. For me, the win isn't changing the whole world. It's proving that the world can still hold space without being redesigned from scratch.

Houdini doesn't need everyone to understand him. He just needs enough people to see him. And that, I've learned, is enough.
Because at the end of the day, Houdini isn't waiting for the world to understand him: he's already living in it, unapologetically. I live it now... half in shadow, half in light, just like him.

Translucent Needs Identified

22. **Social Perception Load** - *Families carry the weight of public judgement when differences aren't immediately visible. Ordinary behaviours spark stares, questions, or blame, forcing constant explanation and defence.*

23. **The Right to Exist Without Explanation** - *Children with translucent needs don't always require new systems, just acknowledgement. Small acts of compassion or acceptance in shared spaces can make daily life easier without a campaign.*

CHAPTER 7

BIAS, BALANCE AND BEING SELFISH

"She calls it selfish, I call it
smart.
You can't pour Wotsits from
an empty packet."

Chapter 7
Bias, Balance, and Being Selfish

Push Houdini's pram through the high street and you'll see it. He's standing up in the seat like a circus cannonball waiting for launch. I'm on my phone, scanning through an email or maybe checking the guards' school app, and to the outside world it looks negligent. Nonchalant. Like I'm one abrupt movement away from sending him flying into next week.

But here's the truth: Houdini is a master of parkour and I'm his sensei. I know his balance points, I know his reflexes, I know where he'll land before he jumps. They see chaos; I see choreography. Still, I know what it looks like.

Then there's the school run. I've accidentally become the benchmark for punctuality. If parents see me en route, they know they're late. Or, worse, they see me attempting the impossible, being on time, and check their watches for reassurance. Being the only Black in the village, I'm sure it doesn't soften the stereotype: we're late. All the time.

And don't even get me started on the reading record. My poor guard's entries don't reflect reality. She reads, she loves reading, but sometimes her record looks bare because I couldn't find a pen in the moment, and once the thought passed, it passed. But to a teacher with twenty-nine other neatly inked records, it looks like neglect. "Black mum doesn't read with her child." Another stereotype reinforced, "If you want to hide something from a Black person, put it in a book."

The bias writes itself. Negligent mother, ironic, isn't it, when she's a bestselling author?

Then there was the hearing test, usual formalities. One of the first questions they asked me was: *"Is English your first language?"* Maybe it was my own imposter syndrome talking, but I couldn't help thinking: did lovely Jane and her son Max, who were mesmerised by Houdini scaling the waiting room walls, get asked that? I doubt it.

I wanted to scream: "My heritage is Jamaican. We speak English. Loudly... You *bomboclaart!"*

But instead, I smiled, gave the polite "Yes," and let the box get ticked. Bias doesn't always shout in the street; sometimes it hides in tick-boxes or whispers in your head, replaying like trauma. It pushes you to perform until there's nothing left. And that's why selfishness became my rebellion.

Because parenting is no different. For mothers, the boxes never end.

These are the biases that are projected on all women, whether parenting Transparent, Translucent or Opaque. And even those without children. If you're a woman you must want kids: check. If you become a mother, you must possess every maternal instinct: check. Because an unchecked box means failure. I too was guilty of the thought until Houdini brought the magic.

As much as you've heard about the lessons in my sacrifices, here's the flip side: Houdini has taught me to be *oh so* selfish. Not mean or stingy selfish. The kind they teach you on planes. First rule of safety: put on your lifejacket and oxygen mask before you help your child.

If you're drowning or can't breathe, you can't save yourself let alone them.

That's me. I put myself first in small but deliberate ways so I'm strong enough to keep showing up. Sometimes it looks like a £7 tub of ice cream, off-limits to the guards because I'm double-dipping. Sometimes it's a music event, a live show, or a long soak with a glass of brandy and a playlist that drowns out the world. Sometimes it's a walk in the park, a night out with the girls or even a date night.

It's not optional; it's survival.

25. Translucent Need: **Parental Self-Preservation**

But selfishness isn't just about ice cream tubs and nights out. Sometimes it's about grieving the pieces of me that got swallowed whole. Before Houdini, I had a career. A desk. An ID badge with my name on it. Team meetings, Friday banter, Christmas parties, even the silly acronyms that made you feel like part of something. Now my title is "full-time carer," and while agencies pay staff with that title a salary and a pension, translucent parents do the same work unpaid, unseen, and sometimes even judged for not pulling their weight.

I miss being called by my actual name. I miss clothes chosen for style instead of practicality. I miss being known for my skills and not just my sacrifices. And I know I'm not alone. Whether single or partnered, every parent in this world eventually hits the wall where career and care collide.

To colleagues, it can look like excuses. "My sister's neighbour's cousin has a kid like that and she works full time." But translucent needs rewrite the rules. They turn a 9-to-5 into six school runs, they turn a team player into "the one who's always off," and they turn ambition into something you tuck into the cracks between appointments.

And maybe that's why selfishness matters. Because when the world strips away the parts of you that made you visible, protecting what's left isn't indulgence. It's survival.

26. Translucent Need: **Career & Identity Sacrifice**

That loss makes the small joys even more vital. So yes, you read right, I said 'Date Night.' I choose oxygen so I can choose them.

I know for many single parents, dating feels impossible. The numbers back it up: some studies suggest that *most* single parents report loneliness after going solo and say anxiety creeps into daily life. These conversations echo in the Mumsnet forums, the Reddit threads, the reels, and conversations at the school gates. For some, the thought of dating feels like carrying extra weight, like you're a burden before you've even said hello.

That isn't my story. I don't carry fear or lack confidence. Imposter syndrome? Maybe. But not fear. Now, I'm single by choice. Don't get it twisted, I've got options. But for me and where I am in my Translucent Parenting journey, being selfish isn't about ridding isolation through companionship, which I know as time passes may become a void that I will seek to fill with more urgency. But for now, I know my village.

So, I try and live in the spaces that keep my fire alive as often as I can. That way, if someone does enter my orbit, it's because they're already attuned to the life I'm building. Because for me, my next will be all about alignment.

You can't be out here searching for love if you haven't even found yourself. That's my focus: to be happy, whole, and already full. And how will I know when the right someone is right? When the happiness I've carved out for myself doesn't shift; it only elevates. And here's why carving out my happiness matters so much.

I started school-runs at twenty-six. With the age gaps between my kids, I've never had a break: one finishing Year 6 as the next starts Reception. With Houdini, my run doesn't end until I'm forty-seven. That's twenty-one consecutive years of the 9am–3pm chokehold. Think about it, twenty-one straight years of signing reading records, doing uniforms and hair on a Sunday: lost water bottles and sticking undesirable pieces of art to the fridge. Most mums of three serve about twelve consecutive years on the school run. My sentence? Nearly double.

So, I claim my days where I can. Half-terms, inset days, summer holidays, they don't always belong to the kids. Sometimes they belong to me. I pre-book dinners, theatre tickets, immersive experiences. My mates can live the spontaneous life; I don't say this begrudgingly, as my age gaps were my choice... although, *someone really should have warned me;* but I can't. Mine takes spreadsheets, babysitters, prep, and my mum.

But I get it done. Because if I don't schedule me in, I disappear. Yet, if you followed me online, you'd think my life looked completely different. My highlight reels are my monthly reminder that if it all stopped tomorrow, I lived today. Otherwise, it is school-runs. Manning the royal quarters. Playing Blind Man's Bluff before bed. Repeat.

But if the average month has thirty days, at least two of them are mine.

Pre-booked. Paid for. Protected.

And that changes everything. Even on the hardest days, the ones where a spare minute to brush my teeth feels like a gift, I can always say: at least I have this coming.

Real Talk

I used to think being a good mum meant erasing myself. Every bias, every whisper, every stereotype had me proving, ticking boxes, performing. But the truth? No one hands out medals for martyrdom.

The only person who loses when I disappear is me, and then, eventually, them. Because the truth? My setup often feels like Groundhog Day. But those two pre-booked days each month remind me I'm still living, not just surviving.

Pep Talk

 To every parent who feels guilty for wanting something of their own: stop. Put on your oxygen mask. Eat the ice cream. Buy the ticket.

Your child doesn't need a martyr. They need a mum who laughs, who still has her spark, who remembers she's more than the paperwork and the pram.

Because selfish isn't betrayal. Selfish is survival.

Reflection

There's no trophy for the mum who sacrifices herself to the last drop.
Burnout doesn't make me stronger; it makes me absent.
Balance is the quiet rebellion. It's how I stay here, fully present, not just surviving the system but surviving myself.

Selfishness doesn't erase sacrifice; it sustains it. Because when I choose me, I'm choosing the version of me that can keep choosing them.

Translucent Needs Identified

24. **Bias Burden** - *Families managing translucent needs also navigate stacked societal biases: race, class, single parenthood, gender expectations; all layered onto an already heavy parenting load.*

25. **Parental Self-Preservation** - *Parents must carve out deliberate time, joy, and rest for themselves. Without replenishment, the weight of care erodes their capacity, turning survival into burnout.*

26. **Career & Identity Sacrifice** – *Translucent Parenting often means stepping out of traditional work. Careers stall, promotions vanish, and financial security takes a hit. Parents also lose identity markers like colleagues, workplace belonging, and social rituals. Unlike paid carers who receive training and recognition, translucent parents do the same labour unpaid, often judged for "not working" or stigmatised for relying on government support. This sacrifice reshapes both income and self-worth.*

CHAPTER 8

THE UNSUNG HEREOS

"They lift her, so she can lift me.
That's what heroes really do."

Chapter 8
The Unsung Heroes

People talk a lot about who failed us. The appointments missed. The forms that broke me. The sideways looks in A&E. And don't get me wrong: those failures shaped me. But this chapter? This one is for the ones who showed up. The ones who hold us up. My unsung heroes.

First, my mum. An angel disguised as a woman walking this earth. My co-parent. The only other human who can handle Houdini's magic without needing a manual.

And here's the part that cracks me wide open: with all my gratitude comes guilt. I was the straight-A student, the careerist, ambitious. Of all her five kids, I never thought I'd be the one who kept her parenting when she should be retiring.

Instead, she's still baby-proofing her home. She buys furniture knowing Houdini will test it. Her weekends become mine to claim. And even though three decades have passed since I was ten minutes late for curfew, her heart still worries in the exact same rhythm. Only difference now? The reasons, not the weight.

And then there are the moments that remind me why she is more than a woman. Like when the other parent cancelled last minute again, and my small slice of freedom, an event I'd planned for months, was about to be ripped away. My mum stepped in, no questions asked. She gathered up the Guards, cooked them dinner, and carried the load so I could carry myself for a change.

But here's the sting: even with all she does, I still worry. If anything happened on her watch, I know she'd carry the guilt like a stone, even though she was only ever helping. And I can already hear the whispers:

"She was where doing what?"
"Her kids were where?"

The same people who think Houdini's needs are caused by the length of my skirt or "bad vibes."

That's the double edge of gratitude: it shines, but it aches.

Then my siblings. My Pitbull. My ribs. My lifelines.

My little sister, always froggy, always ready to jump. We share the same birthday. Rare, yes, but more than rare, it's a sign written in every crevice: you are my person. She sees the silent battles I fight for Houdini, and I see the silent ones she takes on to protect me.

My big sister, the example. The one who wrapped her arms around us all, no judgement, no commentary, just love. You carry the thread that holds the stitching.

My brother, so good I named my son after him. He's my superhero without a cape. Every time I called, he came. Every time. He makes my front door feel like the entrance to my childhood bedroom, showing up with a toolbox, a bar of Galaxy and my favourite flowers, just to remind me of who he sees: me before the chaos.

My elder sister, one above me, I see your translucencies, and I love you for them.

My nieces and nephews, my name-changers. Proof I'm still the favourite aunt and still "cool," even when the guards don't think so. And just like they renamed me, they renamed him. To them, he is not just Houdini, he is *Baby Houdini*. Even if the age gap is a year, the "baby" never drops.

It is their way of wrapping him in both awe and protection, like a title only they get to use. They have also become the unofficial back-up Guards, clocking his moves with the same vigilance as my eldest two. When he vanishes, the cousins join the chorus: "Where's Baby Houdini?" not a complaint, but duty and pride.

My cousin, my left, my warrior of life, proof I can always lean left when things don't feel right. You feel for me before I even feel for myself.

And my Sisters-from-Other-Mothers-and-Misters, thank God calls aren't charged by the minute because those conversations? Therapy. Survival. Lifelines.

And to my step-sister, you deserve a chapter of your own. A single mum raising three, translucent and transparent, with a strength that humbles me. I've been your Karen, tossing the *"why don't you…?"* questions that miss the truth. Because the truth is, no one I've ever met could do what you do. If there's one gift I'd give you, it's permission to be selfish… because you deserve it most.

27. *Translucent Need:* **The Village Safety Net**

My family are my roots, my constants, but heroes aren't always bound by blood. Some arrive in uniforms, in fleeting kindnesses, or in places you least expect.

The Police officer who saw love instead of neglect. The health visitor who listened and acted early. The parents who scoop up my guards, the neighbour who sends gifts, the mum in the park who just got it, and the supermarket worker who guarded the pram while I chased Houdini down aisle four.

They're not saints, not saviours, just everyday people choosing kindness over judgement. Everyday angels hiding in plain sight.

The bloggers, some raw and unapologetic, reminding me I'm not alone; others glossy, reminding me that online glitter isn't gold either. The school friends who treat my kids like kids. The burns specialist who spotted bias before I had to ask. The teachers who send updates written like they actually see him.

They might be rare, but they are there. And they matter.

And then, my gratitude even stretches to the people who aren't there. The ones who dipped out. The ones who didn't show up. Because their absence? It showed me the size of the space I can fill myself.

That's the secret superpower: when the world shrinks around you, you find out just how large you can expand.

Real Talk

F the ones who aren't here. My worth isn't in who left, it's in who stayed. And those who stayed? They get the magic. The alchemy. The ever-expanding light of Houdini.

Pep Talk

So, here's yours: don't just look at who failed you. Start a list of who held you.

The people who step in quietly. The ones who don't need thanks but deserve it anyway. The ones who love you for your personality, not your problems.

Find them. Honour them. Hold them close. Because translucent parenting will stretch you to your thinnest, but your heroes, your guardrails, are the ones who stop you from shattering.

Reflection

My unsung heroes are the reason this story isn't just trauma and bureaucracy. They are the evidence that even in chaos, love survives. If Chapter 1 was about translucency, this one is about clarity, the clarity that nobody raises a Houdini alone.

Your village doesn't have to look like mine. It might be grandparents, in-laws, neighbours, teachers, colleagues, church folk, or even online friends you've never met in person. Whoever shows up for you, that's your safety net. That's your proof you're not carrying this alone.

I know some of mine have cried reading this. Even though they already know it all; it's our group chat with commas, but gathered in one breath, it'll still make them cry. Because they see me. They see Houdini. They see the guards. And they love us still.

That's the gift they carry, they don't just support us; they expand with us. They've stood in the fire and still chosen love. My roots, my constants, my lifelines, they're the proof that Houdini's magic is never just mine to hold. It's shared, it's witnessed, and it's celebrated.

A messy weave of hands and hearts, holding us where others abandoned the load.

Translucent Needs Identified

27. **The Village Safety Net** - *Support doesn't always look the same. Whoever shows up with presence or kindness becomes part of the net that keeps families afloat.*

CHAPTER 9

OUTRO: FINDING MY VOICE

"Hear me where sound isn't; between the swing and the smile."

Finding My Voice

I used to live in fear. Fear of systems, fear of stares, fear of missing something and it all collapsing. And then the day came when everything I feared actually happened, and guess what? Nothing happened. I'm still here. Still standing.

Children like Houdini shape parents into something different, not perfect, but purposeful. I've always been a chatterbox: talk first, think later, an opinion on everything. And yet, I never really had a voice. Words of affirmation are my highest love language, but the strongest love I've ever felt came without words. One thing Houdini has taught me is this: he will never find his voice in the world if I don't find mine.

Thank you for hearing me.

I'm not religious, but I am deeply spiritual. I believe in the laws of the universe: polarity, synchronicities, cause and effect, alchemy, metaphysics. I believe nothing, not even the direction a leaf blows, happens without reason or influence.

So, it feels right that this is Chapter 9. In numerology, nine represents completion, endings that make way for beginnings, cycles closing so new ones can open.

This book was never about a happy ending. It's about clarity. Completion doesn't mean the chaos is done; it means I've reached a point where I can carry it, name it, and still stand.

And yes, more challenges will come. As he grows in strength, my body may weaken. As diagnoses are named and therapies introduced, new systems will open up and with them, new barriers. Teachers, parents, each with their own opinions. My career break may end, or it may shift into something else. New love and new support may enter our lives.

But here's the truth: none of it changes who he already is. His worth has never depended on whether he talks, or when. Even if he never speaks a word, he is still perfect.

Real Talk

I used to think survival meant silence. That if I just kept my head down, ticked the boxes, and played the part, the world would spare me. It didn't. The meltdowns still came, the systems still failed, the stares still burned.

But somewhere between the paperwork and the park benches, I stopped waiting for permission to speak. My child's voice may sound different, or not come at all, but mine? Mine matters. Not because it's perfect or polished, but because it's real. Because if I don't say it, who will?

Reflection

This isn't the story of perfection, or even resolution. It's the story of translucency. Of being seen and unseen, strong and fragile, exhausted and resilient, all at the same time.

If you've made it here, maybe you've seen yourself in the cracks. Maybe you've seen your own translucent needs, or your child's, reflected at you. If so, then this wasn't just my voice. It was ours.

I used to think finding my voice meant sounding brave. But it doesn't. It just means saying the thing out loud, even when your hands are shaking.

Especially then.

Somewhere in these pages, that voice found shape, not only as a mother but as a writer. It learned to hold space for truth without apology, to turn chaos into language, and silence into witness.

The same voice now stands a little steadier, a little surer, no longer asking for permission to exist.

Because I've learned that when you talk, some will choose to say you are speaking

And I'm finally at peace with that.

Pep Talk

 So, here's what I'll leave you with:

- You don't need to fix the entire world to raise your child.

- You don't need to erase your fear; just learn that even when it shows up, you can still survive it.

- And you don't need a petition to prove your child's worth. Presence alone is powerful.

Because translucent parenting doesn't end when this book ends. It continues, every day, in every home like mine: messy, chaotic, beautiful, and enough.

And maybe that's the final point. This isn't the last word. This is only the first word of many more. Because as his story unfolds, so will mine. And the places this book may take me, the lives it might touch? Some things to come may be beyond my wildest dreams. That, in itself, is what keeps life exciting.

Now close this book and go celebrate your own tiny win … because even the smallest light is still magic.

APPENDIX I

THE WORDS I WISH I HAD

"My silence isn't empty. It's full of words I've left for you."

From Me to You – *The Words I Wish I Had*

If you've made it this far, here's my gift to you. Not another leaflet, not another long-arse form, but something real: a pocket of words. A cheat sheet. The phrases I wish I'd had when I first sat across from a doctor, a teacher, or even my own family.

Not jargon. Not clinical. Just lived. Translated. Words you can lift straight into a meeting, a WhatsApp chat, or even onto a form when you're too tired to sound "professional."

Because sometimes the hardest part isn't surviving translucent parenting. It's explaining it.

So here it is the shortcut. The survival tool. The "Karen defence kit" if you will. Use it how you need: print it, screenshot it, highlight it, or just whisper it to yourself when the world makes you feel unseen.
It's not perfect. It's not official. But it's ours.

And if it helps you survive even one waiting room, one sideways look in Tesco, or one unsolicited TED Talk at the swings? Then job done

How to Use the Translucent Needs

What they are:
Short, plain-language signposts for patterns you live every day. They're descriptive, not diagnostic. Use them to make the invisible visible...fast.

When to use them:
Before appointments (GP, SALT, CAMHS, school SENCO, EHCP meetings). In forms (DLA, school questionnaires, referral paperwork). In everyday life (sharing with family, childminders, clubs). For yourself (to track what's changing).

How to read them – *(Each Need pairs:)*
- A name (e.g., Elopement Risk)
- A plain explanation (what it looks like)
- And everyday impact (what it costs the family/system)

You don't have to use all 27. Pick the 3–5 that describe this week.

Quick start (3 steps)
1. *Circle your top 3 Needs right now.*
2. *Add one concrete proof for each (date/time + what happened).*
3. *'**Because of** (Need), **we need** (Support) **by** (When).'*

In the room: scripts you can borrow:

- *"I'll use plain terms so we don't lose the picture. We're dealing with [Need].*
Here's what that looks like this week..."

- *"Because of Elopement Risk, we need a door alarm at nursery by half-term."*

- *"These Needs are descriptive, not diagnostic."*
- *"Right now we're living it daily. What can we put in place this term?"*

On forms (DLA/EHCP/referrals) One Need = one paragraph.

Use this shape:

- *Name the Need*
- *Show it (3 facts, no adjectives)*
- *Impact (time, cost, risk)*
- *Support required (what + who + when).*

Language Swap (plain → professional)

- Runs off without warning → *Frequent elopement; lacks hazard awareness*
- Won't eat most foods → *Sensory-based food aversion; gag response*
- Doesn't look at people → *Limited social reciprocity*
- Doesn't feel pain → *Elevated pain tolerance; delayed injury reporting*

Safety first

If your top Need is Elopement Risk or High Pain Threshold, start there in every meeting. **Risk trumps everything.**

Balancing family load

- When Male Presence & Denial or Absent-Parent Load are active:
- 'Hands-on support is currently single-carer; siblings absorb safety roles.'
- Translate to provision: 'We need respite hours / key worker / transport assistance.'

What good looks like

- You're asked for examples, not excuses.
- Actions are time-bound.
- Support matches risk, not eloquence.
- You leave with who does what by when, in writing.

If it stalls

- 'Please note in the record that support for [Need] was requested today and not agreed, and why.'
- 'What interim measure keeps him safe this week while we wait?'
- Please record who will follow-up and the date.

Keep The Heartbeat

Repeat this line whenever it gets clinical:

"These Needs are here so he can be seen, not sized. We're asking for recognition, not a label."

Top 3 Needs Worksheet

Need #	Name	Impact	Risk	Support Requested

The Translucent Needs: *Quick Guide*

1. **Sensory Seeking Behaviours**
   Kids may reject clothing or textures and instead seek regulation through movement: swinging, climbing, spinning, or jumping. These repetitive actions help manage discomfort in their bodies.

2. **Motor Extremes**
   Strength, speed, and force often go beyond typical limits. Proprioception (body awareness) can be off, leading to fearless climbing, crashing, or boundary-testing that looks superhuman.

3. **Risk Tolerance & Thrill-Seeking**
   Drawn to high-intensity play, they may underestimate danger. What looks reckless is often a drive for sensory input and control.

4. **Parent Sensory Load**
   Caring for heightened sensory needs amplifies your own stress. Constant noise and vigilance overload your system, demanding coping strategies just to stay present.

5. **Social & Communication Style**
   Instead of seeking people, some focus on objects, repetitive play, or routines. Eye contact, greetings, and back-and-forth play may be limited.

6. **Parent Communication Strategies**
   Parents often rely on humour, quick scripts, or deflection to manage judgement. These protect your child's dignity, and your energy.

7. **Stimming & Repetitive Behaviours**
   Hand-flapping, rocking, or spinning objects are regulation tools. They release emotional tension and anchor children in unpredictable spaces.

8. **Vocal Stimming**
   Speech-like sounds, babbling, or repeated vocal rhythms provide the same regulation as physical stims. To outsiders it may sound

like nonsense, defiance or even speech, but it is expression in its truest form; communication through sound, cadence, and energy.

9. **Sleep Avoidance & Regression**
   Sleep can shift in two directions. Some children use it as a retreat from overstimulation or social demands, while others find rest difficult because their bodies remain highly alert. Even with routines, baths, or weighted blankets, sleep may not come easily, and nights can stretch into unsociable hours for everyone caring for them.

10. **Bias & Coping Overlap**
    Families may face stereotypes layered onto the load: race, class, or culture stacked on top of parenting. It's not just needs; it's perception.

11. **Emotional Resilience & Empowerment**
    Parents have to affirm their child's worth even when the world doesn't. Advocacy becomes empowerment, finding strength in vulnerability.

12. **Digestive & Environmental Impact**
    Restricted diets can cause internal imbalances, resulting in stools with extreme odours. The smell permeates the home, needing bins outside and constant ventilation.

13. **High Pain Threshold**
    Injuries and illness may not be shown in typical ways. Kids may keep playing despite burns, cuts, or fevers, making vigilance critical.

14. **Elopement Risk**
    A tendency to bolt or wander without danger awareness. Everyday spaces quickly become high-risk zones.

15. **The Language Barrier**
    Parents describe lived chaos in plain words; professionals reduce it to jargon. Humanity gets lost in translation.

16. Limited Social Reciprocity
Responses to names, greetings, or gestures may be reduced.
Families learn subtler cues of connection outsiders often miss.

17. Measurement Mismatch
Tick-box toys and targets don't always match how our kids play.
When the tools miss the way they really engage, the system reads
absence instead of presence, and compliance instead of truth.

18. Sibling Adaptation
Siblings explain differences, carry responsibilities, and sacrifice
parts of their own childhood to normalise life.

19. Male Presence & Denial
Fathers or male carers may minimise or avoid needs out of pride,
fear, or denial. Sometimes it's not absence... it's silence.

20. Absent-Parent Load
When one parent isn't hands-on, the weight shifts. Siblings,
grandparents, and communities take on roles never meant for
them.

21. Food Aversion due to Sensory Processing
Textures, smells, or flavours trigger fight-or-flight at meals.
Nutrition takes a backseat to survival.

22. Social Perception Load
Families carry public judgement when needs aren't visible.
Ordinary behaviours spark stares, questions, or blame.

23. The Right to Exist Without Explanation
Children don't always need systems redesigned, they need
acknowledgement and compassion in shared spaces.

24. Bias Burden
Race, class, gender, or single-parent stereotypes pile onto the
existing load, shaping how families are perceived.

25. Parental Self-Preservation
Parents must carve out joy and rest for themselves. Without
replenishment, survival slips into burnout.

26. Career Sacrifice & Identity

Parenting children with translucent needs often ends careers. What looks like "not working" is actually unpaid full-time labour, costing parents income, identity, and the simple dignity of being seen as more than "mum or dad."

27. The Village Safety Net

Support doesn't always look the same. Whoever shows up with presence or kindness becomes part of the net that keeps families afloat.

These aren't medical notes. They're plain-language signposts. Descriptive, not diagnostic. They make the invisible visible… quick.

APPENDIX II
MINI TASKS

"You watched my world; now build yours.
Try something new, that's how magic grows."

Mini Tasks:
(Optional, If You Want To Try Something Practical)

These aren't prescriptions. They're small, reflective prompts you can pick up if you want to turn the stories into something active. They sit here as extras, not inside the chapters, so the book still flows as memoir first. If all you want is the story, you can leave this section behind. If you're looking for something to try, each task is simple: one line to write, one thing to notice, one small act that keeps you moving.

Think of them as reminders that survival itself is achievement. You don't need to finish them all. Even one can change how you carry the load.

Chapter 1: The Hidden Chaos

Task: Note the Bad Days

- Write one line about the hardest moments as they happen.
- Use these notes later to describe day-to-day challenges in forms or meetings, so you don't miss the areas that weigh on you most.
- Remember: chaos is not failure. Chaos is evidence you showed up.

Chapter 2: Silent Houdini

Task: Safety First Statement

- Write one sentence that highlights your child's biggest safety concern in each environment: home, school, family, friends, community.
- Lead with safety in every meeting and plan. Major risks deserve professional backing, such as a home safety assessment from an Occupational Therapist, which can support adaptions or funding applications.
- Remember: safety comes before every other need. When risk is recognised, support follows.

Chapter 3: Paperwork Prison

Task: Paperwork Armour

- Build a grab-folder, digital or physical, with reports, forms, and letters. Even taking photos of key pages, written statements, and important dates and storing them in a phone folder or emailing them to yourself reduces the risk of losing proof.
- Use the *Translucent Needs Guide* to shape your statements. Pair plain-language descriptions with system jargon so your child's reality is clear and recognisable.
- If the load is too heavy, ask for support. Friends or family can help organise, and community services or Citizens Advice may help directly or signpost you to specialist support.

Task: **Family Respite Plan**

- Create small moments at home: plan an activity during nap time such as baking, a TV show together, or hot chocolate and a chat. These count as respite too.
- List three ways others can step in for longer breaks such as a few hours of care, an outing for siblings, or providing a cooked meal. Keep the list ready to hand when someone offers help.
- Explore wider support for siblings. Citizens Advice and charity websites may signpost you to discounts, incentives, or family-wide activities.

*Sometimes simply spending time to notice or research their individual interests is the most powerful way to show that they are seen outside of their caring role.

Chapter 5: Tiny Wins

Task: **Merit Chart for Parents**

- Create your own achievement milestones:
  - *Laughed once = 1 point*
  - *Handled an awkward conversation = 5 points*
  - *Asked for help = 10 points*
  - *Faced a meltdown but found laughter within 24 hours = 20 points*

- For visual learners, create a rewards or merit chart similar to the ones we use to support positive behaviours in children. These charts can support a positive mind.
- However you choose to record them, stack your points like rent money. They are proof of progress, because who you were yesterday sure as hell isn't who you are today.

Task: **Your Outside Toolkit**

- Use the ***Translucent Needs Guide*** to prepare short statements and to remind yourself of key safety risks before stepping into public spaces.
- Look out for SEN-friendly sessions such as cinema screenings, soft play, or theatre performances that reduce pressure and make outings easier.
- Carry a "go bag" with essentials like snacks, headphones, comfort items, and wipes. A lanyard or hidden-needs badge can also help signal needs quickly without long explanations.

And if someone stares or comments during a meltdown, point them towards customer services and carry on.

Chapter 7: Bias, Balance & Being Selfish

Task: **Self-Indulgence Log**

- Start with two days out of every thirty that are just for you. Book them in advance and treat them as survival time. These could be a fitness session, a trip to the sauna while the kids are at school or nursery, or any activity that reminds you who you are outside of parenting.
- Use your village to support these plans. Confirm childcare, give notice for babysitting, and always have a backup plan ready such as another sitter, a trusted friend, or time at their house if needed.
- Once a week, add smaller rewards to your Tiny Wins chart such as a favourite meal, a face mask, or music in your headphones. Let these selfish moments act as rewards and let them release the guilt.

Chapter 8: The Unsung Heroes

Task: Record Your Village

- Start a list of everyone who holds you, from family and friends to the shopkeeper who adapts their service, the teacher who notices, or the mum at playgroup who checks in.
- Include your invisible supports too: online forums, bloggers, comment sections, or daily posts that remind you you're not alone and give you ideas or hacks that keep you going.
- Add professionals and peers who step in when needed, such as social workers, community staff, or neighbours who give lifts, meals, or a moment's distraction.

The people who step in quietly. The ones who don't need thanks but deserve it anyway.

Chapter 9: Finding My Voice

Task: Set Your Goal

- Choose one thing just for you in the next three months. It could be journaling, booking an outing, or resting without guilt. Your child's translucency doesn't erase your right to light.
- Make it SMART:
    - **Specific**: Be precise. *"I want to go to the theatre on August 5th to see the new show in London with _____."*
    - **Measurable**: How will you track progress? Booked tickets, saved dates, outfit planned.
    - **Achievable**: Is it realistic in cost, time, and practicality? If not, adjust and restart at "Specific."
    - **Resources**: What do you need? Money (how much and from where), assistance (who and for what, e.g. babysitter, company), equipment or access.
    - **Timeframe**: Is the time given enough? Set checkpoints to review progress. If it is not working at the check-in, reset "Specific" and work back through SMART.
- Treat this as survival, not luxury. A clear, structured goal is proof that you exist outside the load and can still choose joy.